Contents

Any words appearing in the text in bold, **like this**, are explained in the glossary.

Why do we need to eat?

Most people eat two or three main meals a day. We eat because we get hungry and because we enjoy the taste of food. At the same time we fulfil one of the body's essential needs – we supply it with the **nutrients** it needs to stay alive and healthy.

Cells

Your body is made up of millions of tiny **cells**. For example, your bones consist of bone cells, and your skin of skin cells. Most cells are so small you need a microscope to see them, but each one is like a miniature factory, working hard to carry out a particular task. To do this, your cells need a constant supply of **energy**. They also need many different chemicals, which come mainly from your food. These chemicals are called nutrients.

This family is eating a meal that contains several different kinds of food – rice, meat, vegetables, bread and milk. Each of these foods contains a mixture of nutrients.

Nutrients

Carbohydrates, **fats**, proteins, **vitamins** and **minerals** are all different kinds of nutrients. Most foods contain a lot of one kind of nutrient but they contain small amounts of other nutrients too. Together nutrients provide energy and materials that the body needs to work properly and to grow. This book is about protein, what it is and how the body uses it. However, your body needs other nutrients as well as protein, so we shall first have a look at how these keep you alive and healthy.

Energy food

Your body's main need is for food that provides energy. Everything you do uses energy; not just running and moving around, but thinking, eating, keeping warm and even sleeping, too. Carbohydrates and fats provide energy. The body uses carbohydrates, just like a car engine burns petrol, and it needs a big supply every day. Foods such as bread, pasta, potatoes and sugar are mainly made of carbohydrates and are your body's main source of energy.

Fats

Fats provide even more energy than carbohydrates. Foods that contain butter, oil or margarine contain fats, and a small amount of them can supply a lot of energy. However, if you eat more carbohydrates or fats than your body needs for energy, it stores the extra as body fat. Some body fat is useful because it helps to keep you warm, but too much body fat can become unhealthy.

Other essentials

Apart from nutrients, your body relies on food for two other essential ingredients – water and **fibre**. You need to drink at least 1.5 litres a day to make up for the liquid you lose. Fibre is the undigested parts of food and helps to keep your digestive system working well.

Importance of protein

Protein is important because you need it to make new **cells**. Each of your cells consists mainly of water and protein. Your body has to repair and replace your cells constantly and, while you are still growing, it has to create millions of extra cells.

Replacing cells

Most of your cells do not live as long as you do. Skin cells, for example, each last only about 25 days. Your body is making huge numbers of cells all the time to replace those that have worn-out and broken down. For example, it makes about 2,300,000 new red blood cells every single second. Red blood cells are manufactured in the **bone marrow** at the centre of some bones and released into the blood. Most kinds of cells, however, are made in the place where they are needed. Skin cells are made in the lower layers of the skin and stomach cells are made in the wall of the stomach.

Through a microscope you can see the dead cells on the surface of your skin. As dead cells flake off, new cells are produced to take their place.

Growing

From the time you are born until you are an adult, your body is continually growing. It grows so slowly that you do not normally notice the change. Even so, while you are a child, your body is having to make millions of extra new cells to produce bigger bones, extra blood and skin, and so on. This means that it is particularly important for children to eat foods that contain a lot of protein.

Protein in food

Meat, fish, eggs, milk, cheese and beans all contain a lot of protein. Your body cannot use the proteins in the form that you eat them. First it has to break them down into separate units. Then your body rebuilds the units into the particular proteins that it needs. If your food does not give you enough **energy**, your body can use the units of protein to make energy instead.

Vitamins and minerals

Your body needs small amounts of some **vitamins** and **minerals** to help it build new cells. For example, calcium is a mineral that makes your bones strong. Cells also need particular vitamins and minerals to work properly. So long as you eat many different kinds of food, you will get all the vitamins and minerals you need.

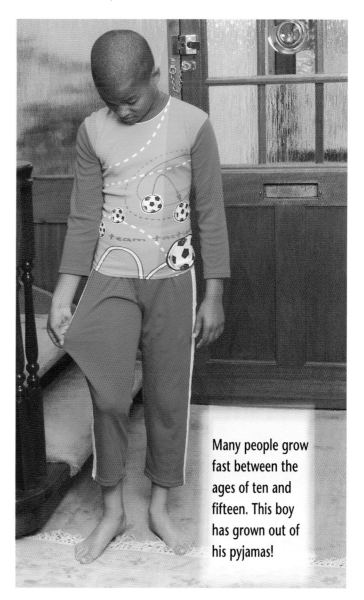

Many people grow fast between the ages of ten and fifteen. This boy has grown out of his pyjamas!

What is protein?

Protein is one of the essential components of living **cells**. There are thousands of different kinds of protein in the human body, in plants and in animals. Proteins in food provide the raw materials from which all the cells in our bodies are built.

Protein in the body

Much of your body is made of different kinds of protein. Muscles, for example, consist mostly of one kind of protein, while bones contain another kind of protein. Hair, nails and the outer layer of skin do not look alike but they are all made of **keratin**. This is a protein that makes them hard and tough. Skin does not feel hard, but it is covered with tough flakes of keratin that make it waterproof. Animals use keratin, too. It is the substance that forms feathers, horns, claws and scales.

Kinds of protein

Your body makes thousands of different proteins from a small number of simple chemicals. It can do this because the simple chemicals are put together in a very complicated way.

Proteins are made up of combinations of smaller units called **amino acids**. Each amino acid is made up of a particular combination of a few simple chemicals.

Hair and nails are both made of the protein keratin. Nails are hard and brittle, but hair is softened by natural oil, which makes it sleek and bendy.

Amino acids

Amino acids all contain the chemicals **carbon**, **hydrogen**, **nitrogen** and **oxygen**. Most also contain **sulphur** and some include **phosphorus**, too. Different amounts of these chemicals combine together in different ways to make various amino acids. Amino acids are the building blocks of proteins.

Chains of amino acids

A protein is made of several different amino acids linked together, rather like beads in a necklace, to form a chain. Each kind of protein consists of a different **sequence** of amino acids. Plants and animals only use about 20 different kinds of amino acids to form these chains, but they can be arranged in so many different ways that they form thousands of different proteins. The beads in a necklace are linked together by a thread, but in a **molecule** of protein, the amino acids are held together by **chemical bonds** called **peptide bonds**.

Protein fact
Most molecules of protein contain around 500 different amino acids, although some have more and others have less.

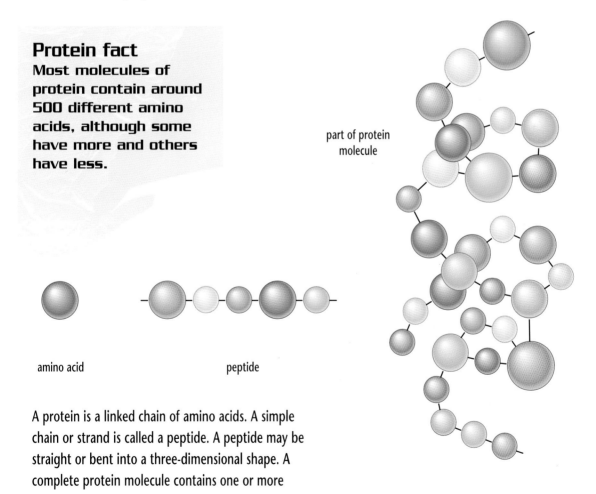

part of protein molecule

amino acid

peptide

A protein is a linked chain of amino acids. A simple chain or strand is called a peptide. A peptide may be straight or bent into a three-dimensional shape. A complete protein molecule contains one or more peptide chains.

Protein from food

All the different proteins in our bodies are made from just 20 different **amino acids**. The body can make eleven of these amino acids itself, but the remaining nine must come from our food. These nine amino acids are called the **indispensable** amino acids because we cannot do without them. Some kinds of food contain much more protein than other kinds, and some foods contain all the amino acids we need.

Passing on protein

Plants make all of their own proteins from the **nutrients** they take in from the soil and from water. When cattle, sheep and other animals feed on plants, their bodies change the plant proteins into animal proteins. This means that food from plants and from animals both contain protein. The muscles of animals, however, are particularly rich in 'indispensable' amino acids. Meat from animals contains all of the nine amino acids our bodies need to be healthy, so animal foods are said to be a complete source of protein for humans.

These foods are all rich in animal protein. They contain all the amino acids that humans need.

Meat

Most of the meat we eat comes from different animals' muscles. When you eat chicken breasts, for example, you are eating the large muscles the bird used to flap its wings. The meat on the legs is the muscle it used for walking. Beef, lamb and pork are mostly the muscles of cattle, sheep and pigs. We cook them and eat them as steak, chops, mince and roast meat. Other parts of animals contain protein, too. Some people eat liver or kidneys, for example. Sausages contain mince, but it is mixed with the ground-up liver, heart and other parts of the animal.

Seafood

Seafood includes fish and shellfish. White fish contains less **fats** than **red meat**, and is a healthy source of protein. The white or coloured flesh of fish, such as cod, haddock, tuna, salmon and sardines, are the muscles that lie along each side of the fishes' backbones. When you eat prawns, shrimps, lobster and other shellfish, you are eating their muscles, too.

Dairy produce

Eggs and milk are also a good source of animal protein. Egg white is pure protein, while the yolk is a mixture of fat, protein and **vitamins**. The milk we drink comes mainly from cows, but cows' milk is also made into cheese, yoghurt and butter. Some yoghurt and cheese is made from sheep's or goats' milk.

Cows spend much of the day and night eating grass. Their bodies turn the proteins in grass into animal proteins of different kinds. They pass those proteins on to us in the form of milk and meat.

Vegetable protein

Although plant protein is called vegetable protein, it comes mainly from plants that we do not think of as vegetables – nuts, cereals and **pulses**. Nuts not only contain protein, but also many **vitamins**, **minerals** and **oils**, as well.

These foods are all rich in protein. For most people, about a third of the protein in their diet comes directly from plants.

Cereals

Cereals are usually eaten as a source of **carbohydrates**, but they contain vegetable protein, too. Cereals include wheat, rice, maize and oats. Wheat is ground into flour and made into bread, cakes and pasta. Breakfast cereals are also a good source of vegetable protein.

Beans, peas and lentils

Different kinds of beans, peas and lentils are called pulses and they also contain plenty of vegetable protein. Some Indian foods, such as dahl, are made from lentils. The Mediterranean dip houmous is made from chickpeas. Beans include broad beans, kidney beans and haricot beans, which are used to make baked beans. Soya beans are a particularly important source of protein.

Soya beans

Vegetarians often use soya beans instead of meat. Many of the vegetarian dishes you can buy in the supermarket, such as vegetarian lasagne and vegeburgers, are made from soya beans. People in Malaysia, Thailand and Japan have used soya beans for a long time. They use it to make foods such as miso and tofu, which are full of protein. Many of these dishes are now popular in the West.

New proteins

You can buy pre-prepared (ready-made) vegetarian meals in shops. Many of these are made from myco-proteins (a kind of **novel protein**). Myco-protein can be grown from **yeast**, other **fungi** or **bacteria**. The myco-protein is **fermented** and then cooked and flavour is added. It can be flavoured to taste like meat, although most vegetarians prefer to add herbs and spices instead of meat flavours.

A complete meal

Even plants that are rich in protein lack one or other of the nine **indispensable amino acids** that we need to get from food. This is not a problem, however, because eating different kinds of vegetable proteins provides the whole range. Many of the snacks and meals you probably already eat contain a mixture. A jacket potato with baked beans mixes two sources of vegetable proteins. Cheese on toast mixes animal and vegetable proteins, as does breakfast cereal and milk.

Peanuts

Peanuts are not really nuts. They grow underground and are more like peas than nuts. Weight for weight, peanuts contain more protein than raw steak and more energy than chocolate biscuits.

Peanut butter sandwiches are a good source of protein. Both the peanut butter and the bread contain protein, and together they supply all the amino acids you need.

How your body digests protein

Your body cannot use proteins in food in the form that you eat them. This is because they are not the exact proteins that your body needs. They contain the right **amino acids**, but in the wrong amounts and in the wrong **sequences**. Food also has to be digested before your body can use the **nutrients** in it. During digestion the food is broken down into tiny pieces that are small enough to pass through the walls of your gut into your blood. Protein is broken down into **peptides** and then into separate amino acids.

Cooking

Apart from nuts, most of the protein you eat has been cooked. Cooked food is softer and easier to chew than raw food. Cooking also kills germs in meat and fish and so makes it safer to eat.

Chewing

Digestion begins in the mouth, when you crunch and chew your food to break it up. As you chew, **saliva** mixes with the food to form a mushy lump. When the lump is soft enough, you swallow and the food passes down the **oesophagus** into your stomach.

In the stomach

The muscles of the stomach act like a slow-moving blender, churning the food around. The stomach juices are strongly acidic and this, together with the churning, turns the chewed up food into a kind of thick soup, called **chyme**. Food usually stays in the stomach for between two and four hours, but some food, such as spaghetti and rice, passes through faster. Food that is rich in **fats** and proteins, however, stays in the stomach for longer.

Stomach juices

The stomach contains a strong acid that attacks the food and kills off germs in it. The acid in the stomach is called gastric juice. It also contains a substance called **pepsin**, which begins to break up the protein molecules into smaller bits (see page 16).

In the intestines

The chyme passes slowly from the stomach into the small intestine. Juices from the liver and pancreas pour into the small intestine. The intestines make their own digestive juices, too. All these juices work on proteins, **carbohydrates** and fats, breaking them into smaller units. The juice from the liver is greenish-brown and is called bile. It breaks up fat into tiny drops.

Breaking down proteins

Chemicals in the juice from the pancreas work on the protein molecules, breaking them down into shorter and shorter strands. Eventually the shorter strands are broken into separate amino acids.

The digestive system.

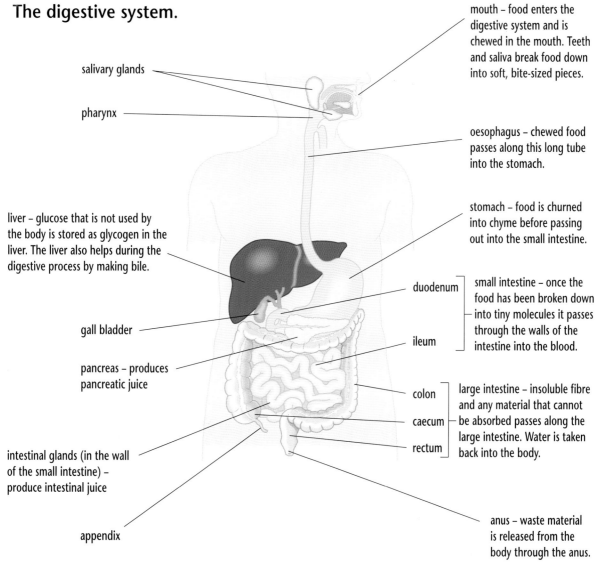

salivary glands

pharynx

liver – glucose that is not used by the body is stored as glycogen in the liver. The liver also helps during the digestive process by making bile.

gall bladder

pancreas – produces pancreatic juice

intestinal glands (in the wall of the small intestine) – produce intestinal juice

appendix

mouth – food enters the digestive system and is chewed in the mouth. Teeth and saliva break food down into soft, bite-sized pieces.

oesophagus – chewed food passes along this long tube into the stomach.

stomach – food is churned into chyme before passing out into the small intestine.

duodenum

small intestine – once the food has been broken down into tiny molecules it passes through the walls of the intestine into the blood.

ileum

colon

caecum

rectum

large intestine – insoluble fibre and any material that cannot be absorbed passes along the large intestine. Water is taken back into the body.

anus – waste material is released from the body through the anus.

Enzymes

Enzymes are the special ingredients in digestive juices that break up large **molecules** into smaller pieces. An enzyme is something that enables a **chemical change** to take place, without being changed itself. In digestion, different kinds of food require one or more different enzymes.

How enzymes work

An enzyme attaches itself like a key in a lock to a particular kind of molecule. In digestion, this makes the molecule split in two. This is the chemical change. The enzyme then separates and attaches itself to another similar molecule. Enzymes work very fast – a single enzyme can split a million different molecules one after the other in just one minute.

Digestive juices

An adult produces about 10 litres of digestive juices every day. Of this, 1.2 litres is saliva and 3 litres is gastric juice.

The right conditions

Digestive enzymes only work in the right conditions. The temperature, for example, must be less that 40° Celsius. The temperature of the body is usually around 37° Celsius – just right for enzymes. Outside the body, food needs to be heated to around 100° Celsius, before it begins to break down. Enzymes allow us to digest food at a much lower temperature.

The enzyme trypsin, which helps to digest protein, is shown magnified here. It is one of the two enzymes in the digestive juices made by the pancreas.

Pepsin

When you start to chew, your mouth produces extra **saliva**. At the same time your stomach produces gastric juices. These juices contain the enzyme called **pepsin**, mixed with **hydrochloric acid**. Pepsin starts to work on the huge molecules of protein, breaking them into shorter strands of **amino acids**.

Enzymes from the pancreas

The digestive juice produced by the pancreas contains several enzymes, two of which work on proteins in the small intestine. They break protein molecules into shorter and shorter strands. They do this by cutting the **peptide bonds** that hold the amino acids together in the chain. These short strands are finally broken into single amino acids.

Babies

When a baby is born, its digestive system has to start working for the first time. It is fed on milk, either from its mother or from a bottle. Babies' stomachs produce an extra enzyme, called rennin. It changes the protein in milk into a solid called casein. This solid takes longer to pass through the intestines, and so gives the other enzymes longer to work on breaking it down.

How enzymes break up protein. In the stomach some of the long chains of amino acids are cut into shorter strands. The process continues in the small intestine where the shorter strands are broken into single amino acids.

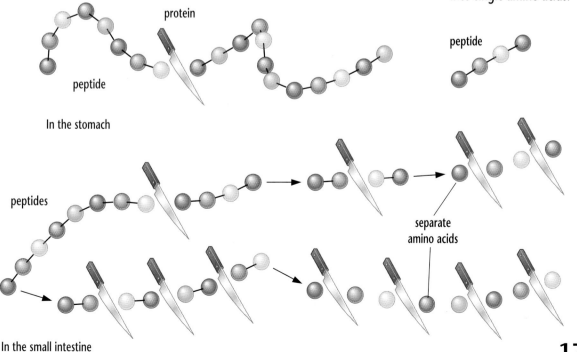

protein

peptide

In the stomach

peptide

peptides

separate amino acids

In the small intestine

Absorbing stuff

Once the **molecules** of protein have been broken down into separate **amino acids**, they pass right through the walls of the small intestine into the blood. The blood takes all the particles of digested food straight to the liver. The liver is an amazing organ that controls hundreds of different **chemical reactions**. One of the liver's many functions is to monitor the level of **nutrients** in the blood, releasing fresh supplies as they are needed.

Through the intestine walls

The surface of the small intestine is lined with millions of tiny bumps, called **villi**. Each villus is only about 0.5 millimetres long and there are up to 40 villi in each square millimetre. These tiny bumps give a much larger surface for digested food to pass into the blood. Their walls are so thin that digested food passes through them into the blood vessels inside.

This magnified photo shows some of the tiny finger-like projections called villi in the small intestine. Nutrients pass through the walls of the villi into the blood.

Body facts

The liver is the largest organ inside the body. When you are resting about a quarter of your blood is held in the liver. Here it is cleaned and processed. Poisons are extracted and destroyed and the blood is restocked with nutrients.

The liver

A vein takes the blood, with amino acids and other particles of digested food, straight from the intestine to the liver. The liver uses some of these nutrients to restock the blood. Your liver can store some excess nutrients, such as sugar, but it cannot store excess amino acids. Instead it changes some of them into sugar and some into other amino acids. The liver then changes any leftover amino acids into a waste substance called **urea**. Urea dissolves in water to form urine and leaves your body through the bladder.

How nutrients reach your cells

Blood, freshly stocked with nutrients, leaves the liver and returns to the heart. The heart sends it to the lungs to pick up **oxygen** and then pumps it through your **arteries** to all the cells in your body.

Undigested food

Not all protein in your food is digested. Some of it gets to the end of the small intestine before it has been broken down into small enough strands to pass into the walls of the gut. Instead these larger strands pass into the large intestine with other undigested food and slowly make their way to the rectum, from where they leave the body as solid waste.

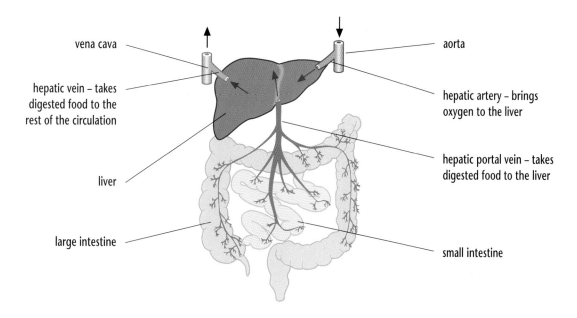

vena cava

aorta

hepatic vein – takes digested food to the rest of the circulation

hepatic artery – brings oxygen to the liver

hepatic portal vein – takes digested food to the liver

liver

large intestine

small intestine

The liver lies just below your ribs on the right-hand side of your body. As blood from the intestines passes through the liver, the nutrients in the blood are processed.

Using protein

The **cells** in the body use protein in several different ways. Each cell takes the **amino acids** it needs from the blood and uses them to build up new proteins. The cell then uses these new proteins to build new cells or to help it carry out its function.

Protein in the cells

Each cell is made up of several specialized parts. Some parts of the cell are particularly concerned with protein. Every cell has **ribosomes** and a Golgi complex. Ribosomes are microscopic factories that make proteins. To do this, they join together the right amino acids in the right order. Different kinds of cells make different proteins in their ribosomes. The proteins are then stored in the Golgi complex. This strange-shaped structure is a kind of warehouse, where the proteins are kept until they are needed. A thin covering, called the cell membrane, surrounds the cell. This membrane is made of protein and **fat**.

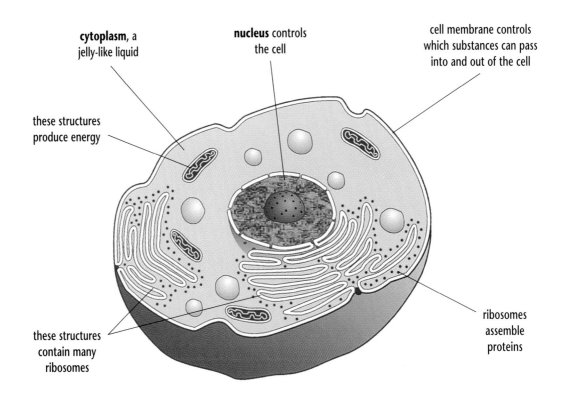

cytoplasm, a jelly-like liquid

nucleus controls the cell

cell membrane controls which substances can pass into and out of the cell

these structures produce energy

these structures contain many ribosomes

ribosomes assemble proteins

Each cell is like a factory with several specialized units. One kind of unit makes protein which is stored in a different kind of unit.

Haemoglobin

Protein plays an essential role in helping your body function properly. Red blood cells, for example, contain the protein haemoglobin. In the lungs, the haemoglobin in red blood cells picks up **oxygen** gas from the air you have breathed in. The oxygen turns the haemoglobin bright red. This bright red blood is pumped by the heart through the **arteries** to different parts of the body. The arteries branch into thinner and thinner tubes called capillaries. The thinnest tubes are so narrow the red blood cells have to change shape to squeeze through them. Here oxygen moves from the haemoglobin through the wall of the capillary and into the cells that need it. As the blood loses its oxygen, it becomes a darker red. Dark red blood returns through the veins to the heart and lungs, where it collects a fresh supply of oxygen.

Collagen

Many parts of your body contain the protein collagen, which is both very strong but also very flexible, or bendy. Collagen fills the spaces between the cells in bones, ligaments, tendons and other tissues in the body. Ligaments are stretchy bands that hold a joint together, but allow it to move. Tendons are similar bands of tissue that attach the muscles to the bones. Collagen is also found in the skin and in the walls of blood vessels. Blood vessels have to be very strong and able to stretch as the heart pumps spurts of blood through them.

Collagen protein provides the structure for your bones, ligaments, tendons and many other parts of your body.

Protein fact

When collagen is boiled it produces a substance called gelatine. This is the substance that makes jellies set and is also used in glues, cosmetics and medicines.

Proteins on the move

Proteins made in some kinds of **cells** are released from the cells to do their work elsewhere. Some proteins, such as **antibodies** and **hormones**, are carried by the blood to other parts of the body.

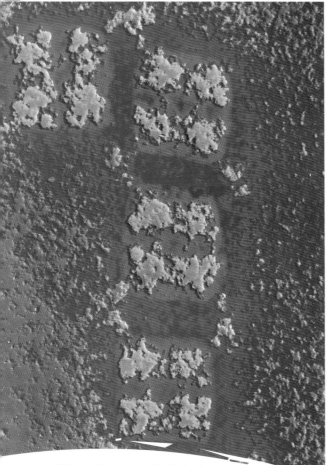

This is what an antibody looks like under a microscope.

Antibodies

Antibodies are proteins that are part of the body's defence against infection. They are made by cells in the **bone marrow**, the red jelly-like substance at the centre of some bones. Each kind of antibody is specially designed to attack a particular kind of **bacteria**, **virus** or poison. Some antibodies attack viruses. They latch on to a virus and make it easier for other blood cells to kill it. Other antibodies deal with bacteria. Even when the infection is over, some of the antibodies remain in the blood. This means that, if the same virus or bacteria invades the body again, the antibody is ready to attack it immediately.

Hormones

Hormones are proteins that work as chemical messengers. They trigger various processes in the body. Each type of hormone is made in a particular gland. For example, the hormone adrenaline is made by two glands just above the kidneys. When you are frightened or alarmed, the glands produce extra adrenaline. Adrenaline prepares the body for action – it makes your heart pump faster and your breathing speed up, and it triggers the liver into releasing more **glucose** into the blood. Other hormones work much more slowly. For example, growth hormone, produced by a gland in the brain, makes you grow taller.

Producing enzymes

Enzymes are made of protein. Different enzymes are used all over the body to speed up different **chemical reactions**. Enzymes in the cells help to build up proteins. Other enzymes in the cells help to turn glucose into **energy**. Some enzymes are used in digestion. The cells of the pancreas, for example, produce two enzymes that break up protein. They are called trypsin and chymotrypsin.

Enzyme facts

Trypsin is one of the enzymes that breaks up protein. It is made in the pancreas, but it is so active it could digest the pancreas itself. To protect itself, the pancreas actually produces a substance called trysinogen. This only becomes trypsin when it reaches the small intestine.

The hormone adrenaline helps athletes perform well. This protein makes them more alert and sends more blood and oxygen to the muscles.

Growing new cells

Amino acids are used to grow new **cells**, either to create extra ones while you are still growing or to replace existing cells. Most of your cells do not live as long as you do. After a while they die and have to be replaced by new cells. In addition some cells may need to be replaced because they have been damaged.

Repairing damaged tissue

When you graze or cut yourself, some of your cells are destroyed and blood leaks out of the capillaries through the broken skin. However, blood contains a protein called fibrinogen. When the blood leaks out and meets the air, the fibrinogen changes into a solid called fibrin that forms criss-cross threads over the wound. The threads slow down the flow of blood, until it **clots** and hardens to form a scab. Under the scab, new cells grow to replace the damaged skin cells. Cells inside your body can become damaged, too. **Bacteria** and **viruses**, for example, damage cells that then have to be replaced.

Growth

Children and teenagers produce the most new cells. The most dramatic rate of growth took place before you were born, when you grew from a single cell to a baby weighing about 3 kilograms and measuring about 50 centimetres long. In the first two years, babies continue to grow rapidly. By the time they are two years old, they have reached about half their adult height! Growth then slows down but continues, sometimes with faster spurts.

Under a microscope you can see the fibrin cells in a wound. This protein helps to seal the wound while new cells are made to replace the damaged ones.

Growth facts

Every human life begins as one cell, produced when a female sex cell is fertilized by a male sex cell. That one cell divides over and over again, forming the different parts of the body. By the time you are an adult that one cell has multiplied into 50 million million cells!

Puberty

Puberty is the time when your body begins to change from a child's into an adult's. It usually starts around the age of eleven or twelve and lasts until about your mid-teens, but this varies from one person to another and differs in girls and boys. During this time you will shoot up in height. You go on growing more slowly until you reach your full height in your late teens or early twenties. Even then your body still makes extra cells. They fill out your shape, making it sturdier and stronger.

How new cells form

New cells are formed by a process called **mitosis**. The **nucleus** in a cell makes an exact copy of itself. The **cytoplasm** inside the cell then divides and forms two cells, each with its own nucleus.

Your body needs to grow new cells as you grow up.

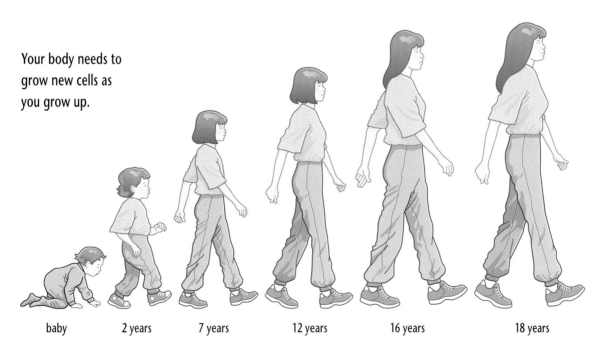

| baby | 2 years | 7 years | 12 years | 16 years | 18 years |

Protein as a source of energy

If the blood contains more **amino acids** than the **cells** need, the liver converts some of them into **glucose**. Glucose is the sugar that provides **energy** for the cells to function. Glucose contains only **carbon**, **hydrogen** and **oxygen**, so the cells break down the amino acids, getting rid of the **nitrogen**, **sulphur** and any other chemical not needed for glucose. The glucose may then be released into the blood to supply the cells. Or it may be changed again, this time into a substance called glycogen. This substance can be stored in the liver until it is needed.

Energy first

It is important to eat a good balance of energy-rich **carbohydrates** and proteins (see pages 36 and 37). If the food you eat does not provide your body with enough energy, then your liver changes amino acids into glucose instead. It does this because the body needs energy more than it needs protein. In some cases, so much protein may be used to supply energy, it leaves the body short of vital amino acids.

Some people eat very few carbohydrates to keep themselves thin. However, when there is not enough glucose (energy-food) in the blood, the liver changes protein into sugar to provide energy instead. When this happens the body may be deprived of vital proteins.

Athletes and body-builders

Athletes may spend several hours every day exercising. The exercise strengthens their muscles and makes their heart and lungs grow larger and work better. Some sports demand a lot of strength or endurance, that is, the ability to keep going. Weightlifting, for example, demands strength, while running a marathon demands endurance. Athletes who take part in these sports often eat a lot of extra protein in their diets, but their diets probably include more than enough protein already. If the extra protein is not needed to build muscle, it will be broken down and used to supply energy instead.

Waste protein

The body can store extra carbohydrates and **fats** to use when it needs them, but it cannot store protein. If you eat more protein than your body needs, the liver will change some of the amino acids into glucose or glycogen, but the rest is lost as waste.

As she exercises, this woman's muscles use some extra protein to become thicker and stronger. Weightlifting develops muscles.

Too much protein

All the cells in the body need protein so they can keep healthy. It is also needed to make new cells. But is it possible to eat too much of this essential body-building substance? The answer is yes! When you consume more energy than you use up, the body stores the excess energy as fat. So too much food, including too much protein, will make you overweight.

The body stores excess **carbohydrates**, **fats** and protein as fat, so eating too much fast food will make you overweight.

Protein waste

The liver processes protein to release the **amino acids** the body needs. If there is an excess of protein it changes some into **glucose**. Then the liver changes any remaining amino acids into a waste substance called **urea**. The process of changing amino acids into glucose produces waste **nitrogen.** This is also changed into urea. As the cells use amino acids they also produce nitrogen as a waste product, and it is taken in the blood to the liver and changed into urea as well.

The kidneys

The kidneys are two organs, one on each side of the spine, just above your waist. As blood passes through them, the kidneys filter the blood and remove urea and any excess water and salt. Urea is a solid, but it dissolves easily in water to form urine. Urine trickles from the kidneys down two tubes to the bladder. Urine is stored in the bladder, which gradually stretches as it fills up. It can hold up to about 600 millilitres of urine at a time. When you urinate, you empty your bladder.

Excess protein

People who take in much too much protein may damage their liver and kidneys. This is because having to deal with the excess protein makes these organs work too hard.

The liver has to work hard to change all this excess protein into urea. The kidneys have to work hard to filter it from the blood.

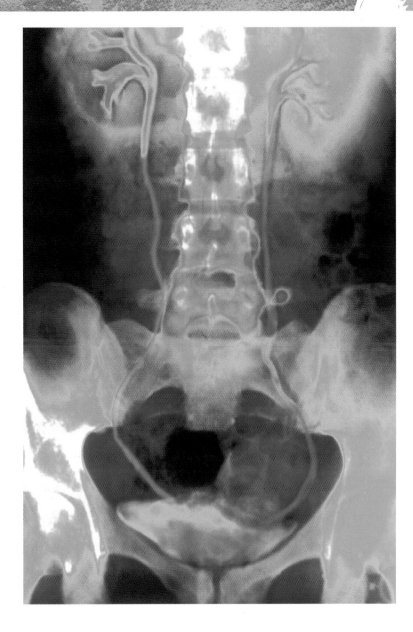

The kidneys process about two pints of blood every minute. The urea and water is filtered out to make urine, which is stored in the bladder before urination.

Urea

Nitrogen is an important **nutrient** that plants need to grow. Urea is rich in nitrogen. It is manufactured artificially and used as a **fertilizer** in gardens and on crops. Urine, however, does not make a good fertilizer since it is too acidic. Artificial urea is also used in cattle feed, plastic and in medicines.

Food allergies

A small number of people react to a particular protein in their food. These are people who are allergic to certain substances, such as the protein in cow's milk, wheat or nuts. Some people are not allergic to wheat, but their body cannot digest it.

Allergies to protein

When a person is allergic to a particular kind of food, their bodies react as though that food were a germ or a poison. Peanuts, milk, cheese, eggs and wheat are the most common cause of food allergy. The most common symptoms of a food allergy are vomiting and an itchy skin rash. Some people may also have difficult breathing. The best way to treat an allergy is to avoid the food that triggers it, but this is easier said than done. People who are allergic to peanuts, for example, cannot eat anything until they have checked the list of ingredients on the label. It is difficult because some foods do not contain peanuts, but might have been cooked in peanut oil. They also need to make sure the food has not touched anything with peanuts in it, for example, in a bakery.

Sharon's story

Sharon is allergic to nuts. When she eats anything that contains even just a small amount of nuts, her body immediately reacts. Within a few minutes, her mouth swells up and she begins to vomit. Her skin breaks out in a red, blotchy rash that is very itchy. These symptoms can last for several hours. Sharon tries to be very careful to avoid eating nuts!

If you are allergic to milk you need to read the ingredients listed on food labels to see if they contain milk.

Gluten

Gluten is a mixture of two proteins and is the substance that makes bread dough stretchy and bouncy. Bread companies sometimes add extra gluten to the dough to make it softer and lighter. Some people's digestive systems cannot handle gluten in the food they eat. In many cases this is not so much an allergy, as the fact that the gluten damages the **villi** on the small intestine. The gluten wears away the villi so that other nutrients may not be absorbed either.

Coeliacs

People who cannot tolerate gluten are said to suffer from 'coeliac disease'. They have to avoid any foods that contain gluten. Wheat has more gluten than other cereals, but rye, oats and barley contain some, too. The only common cereals that are gluten free are rice and corn.

All of these foods contain wheat. People who suffer from coeliac disease cannot eat any of them.

Extreme shock

Some people are so allergic to a particular food their bodies go into extreme shock, also called **anaphylactic shock**. Their blood pressure drops, they become unconscious and, unless they get medical help at once, they will die. Foods that are most likely to cause extreme shock are nuts, shellfish and eggs.

Too little protein

Most people in **developed countries** do not have a problem in getting enough protein. In fact most people in these countries eat more protein than they need. Only people who have problems with diet, such as those with eating disorders, like **anorexia** or **bulimia**. Most people who suffer from a lack of protein live in **developing countries**.

Protein deficiency

Many people in developing countries do not have enough money to buy meat, eggs or other food that contains protein. Children and babies are most affected by not getting enough protein. It affects them in several ways. One of the first signs is that they cannot resist disease as well. Their bodies are also less able to replace worn out or damaged **cells**, so it takes longer for cuts and wounds to heal. They may feel ill all the time and they cannot learn as well. They do not grow as tall as they should, because their bodies cannot build all the extra cells required for growth.

Kwashiorkor

A severe lack of protein leads to a disease called kwashiorkor. It affects mainly young children who have stopped getting milk (which is full of protein) from their mother and are then fed solid foods that lack protein. In the villages and countryside in much of Africa, the Caribbean and the Pacific Islands, babies, like everyone else, are fed on yams, cassavas, sweet potatoes and green bananas – foods that are rich in **carbohydrates** but low in protein.

Symptoms of kwashiorkor

One of the most obvious signs of kwashiorkor is a large, swollen belly. The swelling can make the baby or child look quite fat. But it is not caused by **fat**, but by liquid that has collected below the skin. The liver also becomes larger. The skin becomes flaky and the hair becomes thinner and loses some of its colour. The baby or child stops growing and becomes irritable, tired and listless.

Pedro's story

Pedro lives in a remote region of Colombia in South America. His usual diet consists mainly of corn and potatoes, and contains very little protein. He had been ill for two weeks, when his body began to swell. His father strapped four-year-old Pedro to his back and walked for five hours to the nearest medical centre. There student doctors told him Pedro had kwashiorkor and he was treated in hospital. Two weeks later he was ready to go home, but the students knew that his family still could not feed him properly and that he would probably never grow as well as he should.

This young child is suffering from kwashiorkor, caused by a severe lack of protein in its food. Children with kwashiorkor will die unless they are treated.

Dying of hunger

Famine is the most extreme case of lack of food. People starve when they do not have enough food to supply them with sufficient **energy** or with proteins. Their bodies become extremely thin and their organs stop working properly. This condition is called marasmus and, unless they find food, they die.

Symptoms of marasmus

People who are starving feel hungry all the time. This is not the sort of hunger that you feel when your stomach rumbles and you are looking forward to a meal. Instead it is a continual pain in the belly and a longing for food. The person loses weight as the body's supplies of **fat** are used up. Then the body converts the protein in muscle into energy. As their muscles disappear, the shape of their bones becomes clearly visible through their skin. Their ability to fight disease is damaged and they often fall ill. Children stop growing and become listless, tired and irritable. The development of their brains is also affected and they find it difficult to learn or think properly.

Growing taller

Many people from poorer countries move to richer countries in order to earn more money. Their children then eat a healthier diet than their parents did when they were young. When the children grow up they are often noticeably taller than their parents.

How tall you grow does not depend entirely on the amount of protein in your diet. These two children are the same age, but are different heights. Some people grow taller because their parents are tall.

34

Treating marasmus

People who have been starved of food cannot eat large amounts at first. They need to be fed with regular small amounts of water that contains sugar and salts. Gradually they may progress to milk and then to solid food.

Mothers and babies

Pregnant women, mothers and young children are most at risk in a famine. Pregnant women have to feed both themselves and the baby growing inside them. Once the baby is born, it may feed on its mother's breast milk for up to two years. Mothers need extra protein so that their babies can grow.

Causes of famine

Although the world can produce enough food to feed everyone, millions of people starve to death every year. Most often, people starve because they cannot afford to buy food, particularly food that contains protein.

Area most likely to be affected by famine

These are the parts of the world that are most likely to suffer from famine. They include countries where people are extremely poor and where there is often no rain for months or years.

Healthy eating

Your diet is all the food you normally eat. To have a healthy diet, you need to eat a variety of different kinds of food to give you all the **nutrients** you need, that is, all the **carbohydrates**, **fats**, **vitamins** and **minerals** as well as the protein you need. Of course, you do not think of food as proteins, carbohydrates and other nutrients, but as bread, fruit, cheese, and so on. The 'Balance of Good Health' divides foods into five main groups and shows how much you should eat from each group every day.

1 – Bread, other cereals and potatoes

This group of foods is rich in carbohydrates. About a third of the food you eat every day should come from this group. These foods also contain vegetable protein and some important vitamins and minerals.

2 – Fruit and vegetables

Foods in this group are rich in vitamins and minerals. About another third of the food you eat every day should come from this group. These foods also contain plenty of fibre, which is not a nutrient, but it helps to keep your digestive system working well. We should eat at least five portions of fruit or vegetables every day.

3 – Meat, fish, and alternatives

Foods in this group include eggs and **pulses.** They are rich in proteins and you should eat two portions of food from this group every day. Some meats, such as lamb and pork, have more fat in them than, for example, chicken or beans. Adults and children who are overweight should try to choose food that contains protein, but is low in fat.

4 – Milk and dairy foods

This group includes milk, cheese and yoghurt. These foods are rich in protein but many also contain quite a lot of fat. Young children especially need to eat some fat, but adults and children who are overweight should look for low-fat varieties. Whole milk has the highest fat content. Semi-skimmed milk has most of the fat removed. Skimmed milk has almost no fat, but it is not recommended for children under the age of five years.

5 – Foods full of fat or sugar

This group includes many popular snacks, such as crisps, chocolate, sweets, biscuits, sweet fizzy drinks, chips and sausages, which are high in fat and sugar. If eaten in excess these foods can make you overweight. You should only eat a small amount of these foods.

Rules for healthy eating
- Eat a wide variety of food.
- Eat most food from groups 1 and 2.
- Eat only a little food from group 5.

This plate of food shows the wide variety of food you should eat to enjoy the 'Balance of Good Health'. It is divided into five main groups of food. The space given to each reflects how much of each you should eat.

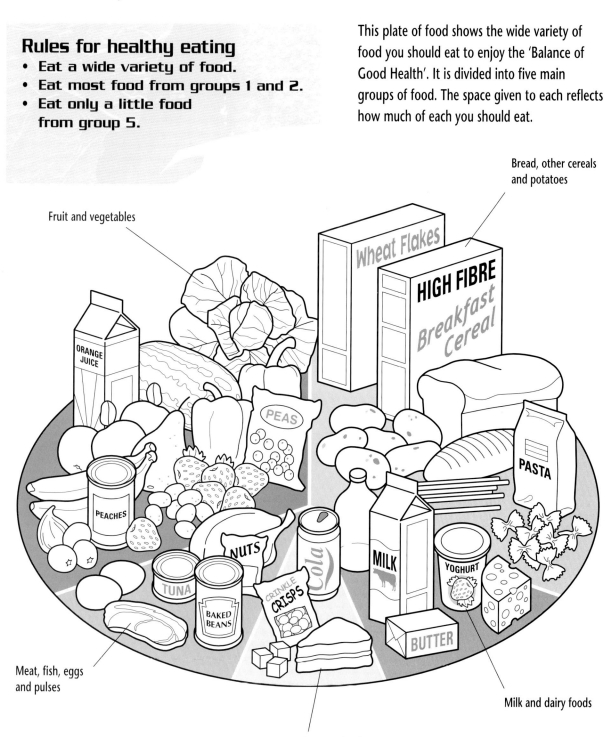

Fruit and vegetables

Bread, other cereals and potatoes

Meat, fish, eggs and pulses

Fatty and sugary foods

Milk and dairy foods

Different kinds of diet

People who live in different parts of the world often eat different foods or prepare food in different ways. Traditional food can be very healthy, because it often uses **pulses** as well as meat. Many people follow diets for religious reasons that deliberately leave out one or several kinds of food. Muslims and Jews, for example, do not eat pork, and Hindus do not eat beef. Vegetarians do not include meat in their diets and vegans do not eat anything that comes from animals at all.

International food

Traditional cooking, from countries such as Mexico, China, India and Thailand, is often very healthy and is now popular in many other countries, too. Their dishes can use strong spices and particular ingredients, such as water chestnuts, okra, and coconut milk, but most of it is based on familiar food – rice, vegetables, chicken, lamb and fish. Food cooked in different ways can be tasty and nutritious.

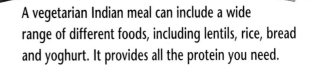

A vegetarian Indian meal can include a wide range of different foods, including lentils, rice, bread and yoghurt. It provides all the protein you need.

Vegetarians

Vegetarians are people who do not eat meat or fish. They do, however, eat animal protein in the form of eggs and dairy products, such as milk and cheese. This is because eggs and dairy products do not involve killing the animals. A vegetarian diet is perfectly healthy, particularly if each meal includes more than one source of protein. This can be done by mixing pulses, such as soya beans or lentils, with rice or bread, or by mixing animal protein, such as cheese or yoghurt, with vegetable protein. A vegetarian diet is often healthier than a meat-eating diet, because it is likely to contain less animal **fats**. It is not healthy to eat a lot of these fats.

Vegans

Vegans are people who do not eat any food that comes from animals – they eat only plants. This means that they do not eat milk, cheese, eggs and yoghurt as well as meat and fish. Most cakes, biscuits, bars and other manufactured products contain milk powder or some animal product and so vegans avoid them, too. A vegan diet can provide all the proteins that people need so long as they make sure to eat protein from more than one source at each meal. Vegans, however, have to plan their food carefully to make sure they get all the **vitamins** and **minerals** they need.

Athletes

Athletes, footballers and other people who play sport do need some extra protein to build up their muscles, but most people eat more protein than they need. Athletes need to include more **energy** food in their diet, but not more protein.

A vegetarian would eat this meal of a jacket potato and cheese, but a vegan would not.

Healthy snacks

Most people have favourite snacks that they eat when they are hungry between meals. Food companies produce a huge range of snacks that many children like. They include crisps, sweets, chocolate bars, biscuits and cakes. Most cinemas sell popcorn and fizzy drinks for people to have while they watch the film. Eating too many of these snacks an be unhealthy because they contain a lot of sugar and a lot of **fat**. But many other snacks are tasty and healthy, too. Here are some that are rich in protein without being unhealthy.

Nuts

Nuts are a good snack to eat with your fingers. Peanuts are particularly rich in protein, but many of the packets of peanuts you can buy are too salty. Look for unsalted peanuts and try other nuts, too, such as cashew nuts, walnuts and pecan nuts. Seeds, such as sesame seeds, sunflower seeds and pumpkin seeds, all contain lots of protein.

Houmous, taramasalata and tzatsiki are traditional dips. They are tasty and rich in protein. You can easily make your own tzatsiki by mixing chopped-up cucumber, onion, mint and garlic into plain or natural yoghurt.

Popcorn

Popcorn is made from corn, which is a good source of protein. The popcorn you buy in the cinema is either very sweet or very salty and costs a lot of money. But it is easy and healthier to make at home, and it is fun too. You buy the raw grain and cook it in a little oil in a pan with a lid. You can hear the corn hitting the lid and sides of the pan as it pops. Don't remove the lid until the grains have stopped popping! While it is still hot, add a little sugar or salt to flavour the popcorn.

Ask before you cook!

If you are going to make your own snacks, ask an adult first. If you are not used to cooking, you may need an adult to help you. If you use a cooker or hob, make sure you turn it off when you have finished.

A toasted cheese and tuna sandwich is a healthy snack. Sandwich toasters get very hot, so ask an adult to help you if you make a snack like this one.

Nutritional information

The top table shows how much protein you need between the ages of 7 and 14. Based on weight, children need more protein than adults. Pregnant or breast-feeding women need more protein than other adults.

Daily requirement of protein

Age	Protein (grams per day)
All 7–10 years	28.3
Boys 11–14 years	42.1
Girls 11–14 years	41.2

The table below shows amounts of particular foods needed to get your daily requirement of protein. The differences between girls and boys are too small to make a difference. It is best to obtain your protein from a variety of foods.

Amounts of foods needed to supply daily requirements

Food	7–10 year olds	11–14 year olds
Milk and dairy food		
Whole milk	1.5 pints (900 g)	2 pints (1300 g)
Cheddar cheese	100 g	165 g
Meat and fish		
Roast chicken	a portion (120 g)	1.5 portions (170 g)
Canned tuna	120 g	180 g
Pulses		
Canned baked beans	1.5 medium cans (550 g)	2 medium cans (810 g)
Boiled lentils	380 g	550 g
Cereals		
Wholemeal bread	a third of a loaf (310 g)	half a loaf (460 g)
Cornflakes	12 portions (360 g)	18 portions (540 g)
Snacks		
Peanuts	115 g	175 g
Milk chocolate	340 g	500 g

This table shows how much protein is contained in 100 grams of a wide variety of foods. It allows you to compare different foods and to work out how much protein is in foods you usually eat.

Average protein content of some foods

Food	Protein (per 100 g)	Food	Protein (per 100 g)
Milk and dairy food		**Meat**	
Milk (full fat)	3.2	Grilled lean, back bacon	25.3
Milk (semi-skimmed)	3.3	Minced beef	23.1
Fruit yoghurt	5.1	Stewing steak	30.9
Cheddar cheese	25.5	Roast lamb	26.1
Boiled egg	12.5	Salami	13.0
		Pork sausages (grilled)	13.3
Cereals		Roast chicken	24.8
White bread	8.4	Roast turkey	28
Wholemeal bread	9.2		
Cornflakes	7.9	**Pulses**	
Cooked spaghetti	3.6	Canned baked beans	5.2
Boiled rice	2.6	Tofu	8.1
		Cooked, dried lentils	7.6
Fish			
Grilled fish fingers	15.1	**Snacks**	
Boiled prawns	22.6	Chocolate biscuits	5.7
Canned sardines	23.7	Peanuts	24.5
Canned tuna	23.5	Houmous	7.6

A homemade cheese and tomato pizza that weighs 720 grams contains 61 grams of protein. If it is shared between four 10-year-old children, it will provide half the protein they need. But if it is shared between four teenage boys, it will provide only about a third or a quarter of their daily requirement of protein.

Glossary

amino acids building blocks of protein. Different amino acids combine together to form a protein.

anaphylactic shock severe form of allergy in which a person's body reacts so strongly to a protein they can die

anorexia eating disorder in which a person eats so little food they become extremely thin

antibody cell that attacks a particular kind of bacteria, virus or poison. It is made in the bone marrow and released into the blood.

antidote something that stops the harmful effects of a poison

arteries tubes that carry blood from the heart to different parts of the body

bacteria single, living cells. Most kinds of bacteria are harmless, but some kinds can cause disease.

bone marrow jelly-like substance in the centre of some bones. Red and white blood cells are manufactured in the bone marrow.

bulimia eating disorder in which a person often eats a lot of food, but then makes themselves vomit

carbohydrates substances in food that your body uses to provide energy. Foods that contain a lot of carbohydrate include bread, rice, potatoes and sugar.

carbon one of the most common elements, or simple substances. All living things contain carbon combined with other elements, particularly hydrogen, oxygen and nitrogen.

cell smallest living unit. The body is made up of many different kinds of cells, such as bone cells, blood cells and skin cells.

chemical bond joining together of two molecules due to their chemical structure

chemical change joining of two substances to produce a different substance, or the splitting up of a substance into two or more different substances

chemical reaction see chemical change

chyme mushy liquid which passes from the stomach to the small intestine. It is formed from partly digested food mixed with the digestive juices of the stomach.

clot when part of a liquid becomes so thick it forms a soft lump

cytoplasm all the material inside a cell except the nucleus

developed countries   wealthy countries that have well established industries and social services, such as transport, education and hospitals

developing countries   poorer countries that do not have well established industries and services, such as transport, schools, welfare

energy   ability to do work or to make something happen

enzyme   substance that helps a chemical change take place faster without being changed itself

famine   lack of food that affects most people in a region. Famine leads to starvation.

fats   substances in some foods that your body uses to provide energy. Fat is stored by your body in a layer below the skin and helps to keep you warm.

fermented   slowly broken down by a fungus, such as yeast, or bacteria to form a new substance

fertilizer   chemical or natural substance added to soil to provide nutrients for plant growth

fibre   in food, the undigested parts of plants

fungi   group of living things that includes mushrooms, yeasts and moulds

glucose   kind of sugar

hormones   substances produced by different glands in the body that affect or control particular organs, cells or tissues

hydrochloric acid   liquid produced when hydrogen and chlorine combine together. An acid tastes sour or sharp.

hydrogen   invisible gas that is one of the gases in the air. Hydrogen combines with other substances to form, for example, water, sugar, protein, fat and hydrochloric acid.

indispensable   so necessary you cannot do without it

keratin   kind of protein that your hair, nails and outer layer of skin are formed of

mineral   non-living substance found in the ground. Your body needs certain minerals to function healthily.

mitosis   process by which a cell divides to form two new identical cells

molecule   smallest part of a substance that can exist and still be that substance

nitrogen   invisible gas that is the main gas in the air. Nitrogen combines with other substances to form, for example, all the different tissues in your body.

novel protein   new kind of protein that is produced from fungi or yeast

nucleus part of the cell that controls all the cell's activities

nutrients parts of food that your body needs to get energy, to build and repair cells, and for the cells to function properly. Nutrients include carbohydrates, fats, proteins, vitamins and minerals.

oesophagus the tube through which food travels from the mouth to the stomach

oil in food, a form of fat found in plants

oxygen invisible gas that is one of the gases in the air. The body needs oxygen in order to break down sugar to form energy.

pepsin enzyme in the stomach that starts to break down proteins

peptide simple chain of amino acids

peptide bond chemical bond that joins peptides together

phosphorus simple substance that is needed for plants to grow

pulses group of foods that includes lentils, peas and beans. Pulses are the seeds of some plants and are rich in protein.

red meat meat such as beef and lamb which are usually dark in colour, although red meat includes pork

ribosomes particles in the cells of the body that build up proteins from amino acids

saliva watery liquid made by glands in your mouth and the inside of your cheeks

sequence several things in a particular order

sulphur simple substance that forms part of most proteins

urea substance formed from waste material in the liver. Urea mixed with water makes urine.

villi tiny bumps in the intestines through which digested food and water is absorbed

virus kind of germ that causes certain diseases. Viruses are smaller than bacteria.

vitamins chemicals that your body needs to stay healthy

yeast kind of fungus. Yeast is used to make bread and alcohol.

Resources

Books

Body Focus: Digestive System, Carol Ballard (Heinemann Library, 2003)

DEFRA Manual of Nutrition, (HMSO, 1995)

Digesting: How we fuel the body, Angela Royston (Franklin Watts, 1998)

Web sites

www.bbc.co.uk/health/nutrition
Nutrition and healthy living are the subject of this part of the
BBC's website.

www.mckinley.uiuc.edu/health-info/nutrit/hlthdiet/smart_snacks.html
Tells you about all kinds of healthy snacks.

www.mckinley.uiuc.edu/health-info/nutrit/hlthdiet/soybeans.html
Tells you about the benefits of soybeans and the products that contain them.

www.NutritionAustralia.org
This is the information website of the Australian Nutrition Foundation.

www.nutrition.org.uk/
Website of the British Nutrition Foundation which gives information on all
aspects of diet, including proteins. Click on nutrients to get started.

Index